Beaded Ornament Covers

Book Two

Sheila Root, PhD
Master Jeweler

©2012 Root's Beads
Root's Beads
3150 Fogarty Ave.
Depoe Bay OR 97341
541-764-5040

www.rootsbeads.com

Sheila Root is a beading artist and co-owner of Root's Beads along with her husband Richard. She has been in the bead business for twenty years and has taught hundreds of students in seed bead techniques and basic and advanced stringing techniques as well as wire techniques. A former university professor with degrees in design and a certificate in Master Jewelry, she has been designing and selling "wearable art" for many years. Sheila also has a background in textile arts and was a founding member of FiberRoots, participated in many gallery exhibitions, was featured artist at the Haymarket Gallery and placed Honorable Mention in a national competition. She has written several books including *Graphics for Interior Space*, *Beaded Ornament Covers*, *Wire Wrapping Stones* (1st edition), *Wire Wrapping Stones and Beads* (2nd Edition) and *Beaded Ornament Covers Book Two*.

Contents

Getting Started

Selecting Ornaments

All ornaments are not created equal. They come in a wide variety of sizes, shapes, colors, materials and finishes.

Ornament covers work best over smooth round balls. Either shiny or matte works well depending on your color selection of beads. Generally you would want to avoid patterned ornaments because the pattern competes with your bead work.

Ornaments now come in both glass and unbreakable plastic. The glass balls have a nicer shine but the unbreakable ones are great if you have kids or pets. All ornament covers in this book are worked with an open bottom so that if a ball gets broken or scratched it can be easily replaced.

Size of the ornament is an important consideration: all the ornaments in this book are worked on round 2 9/16 inch balls, just over 2.5". This is a standard size that is always readily available during the holidays. Stock up after Christmas when they are on sale so that you will be prepared for your next season's creations. If you use a larger or smaller size ball all the bead counts will have to be adjusted to fit.

The neck size of the ornament is also important. The ones used in this book all have a neck that is about ¾ inch in diameter. If the neck on your ornament is a bit smaller the cover will still fit; if it is bigger then you will need to make adjustments to the top ring.

Selecting Beads

Like ornaments, not all beads are created equal either.

The main body of most ornament covers is made up of seed beads. Seed beads are made in a variety of sizes and shapes and in several different countries. These ornament patterns use Miyuki and Toho rocailles (round seed beads) made in Japan. These beads are very uniform in size and have good sized holes so you don't get your needle stuck so easily. If you use any other brand of seed beads you may need to adjust the pattern. Seed beads made in the Czech Republic tend to be smaller even though they are technically the same size. If you use them you may find that the finished ornament will not go over the ball unless you have adjusted the quantities. There is also another Japanese seed bead maker whose beads are larger than the Miyuki and Toho seed beads, making your cover too loose. Seed beads are also made in Taiwan, China, and India. They are less expensive but much more irregular which can ruin the final appearance of you ornament cover. **Try the cover on your ornament frequently as you work to make sure the size fits correctly!**

Size 15/0 rocaille seed beads are quite small and not everyone likes to work with them. However, they are what make your ornament cover lay properly on the ball and give you details and drape that you can't get with larger sizes. Any place that you have more than one strand entering at the same place there should be at least one 15/0 on each strand next to the intersection so that it does not become too bunchy and leave threads showing. In this illustration the dark beads and the center gold bead are 11/0 but the tiny gold beads are 15/0 so that the joint lays flat.

Bugle beads are often used in ornament covers as well. Bugle beads are a long bead, either straight or twisted. The twisted ones give a nice sparkle in ornament covers and catch the lights when hanging on a tree. Since bugle beads are a "cut" bead that means that the ends are going to be sharper than other seed beads. When working with them you want to pull

your thread snug but not so tight that you cut the thread against the sharp end of the bead. The Japanese bugle beads tend to be a little less sharp than other brands.

Beads for fringe are easy; just about any bead that the needle will go through twice will work. Usually you want beads that are a little bigger to give the fringe weight so that it hangs properly. Teardrops, crystals, fire polish beads, and pearls (man made, not natural fresh water pearls-holes are usually too small) all work well.

Tension

Keep the tension on your thread tight enough that you don't have loose spots of bare thread showing. Do NOT pull the thread so snug that you cut it on the bugle beads or make the ornament cover stiff. Covers need just a bit of softness in the tension to hang nicely.

Needles

All the ornaments in this book were worked with size 10 beading needles. It is always easier to use the largest size of needle you can because they are easier to thread and bend less. It doesn't hurt to have a few other smaller sizes available though just in case you get into a tight spot. Always work with a single thread, not doubled, so that you can change the needle if needed and have more room inside the beads to accommodate several passes of thread.

Beading needles are the longer ones, about 2" long. The length is helpful when running the needle back through a section of beads. Sharps are the short needles, about an inch. Keep a couple of sharps on hand so that if you end up with a really short thread you can still put a sharp on it to weave it back into the cover.

Thread

Nylon beading thread works very well for ornament covers. It is a flat thread that is easy to thread into a needle, fits easily through the beads and is very strong with almost no stretch. It comes in pretty colors so you can select the color that goes best with your beads. Choose a color that blends in well so that it doesn't show at the intersections. If your beads are transparent choose a color that doesn't leave a line through the beads. Note that in this book there are some covers that use a thread darker than would have been desired so that the thread is more visible in the photos. The samples were all worked with Superlon brand.

Avoid sewing thread. It is a spun thread that will not hold up for bead work. Also do not use fishing line. It is too wiry and is designed to break down over time so that it doesn't pollute the environment but you don't want your lovely ornament covers to break down over time after all that work!

Condition your thread. Conditioning the thread helps to keep it more manageable when you are using a long length and helps prevent fraying. The newer synthetic thread conditioners work better with nylon thread than old fashioned bee's wax. Bee's wax tends to gum up. The synthetic conditioners have silicone which gives the thread a more slippery feel.

Work with as long a thread as manageable but not more than about five feet or you will just get tangled up. You can not possibly make a whole ornament cover with one thread but you also don't want to have to add more thread any more often than necessary. Whenever you start a new thread, tie it on and leave about six inches so that you can get it back on a needle to weave the end in later. Leave the end until you have worked a ways past it, then go back and weave it in. When ending a thread, work it back into the ornament tying several half hitch knots to secure it before cutting off any excess. If the thread end is very short, switch to a shorter needle to give you more room to make your knots.

Ladders

"Ladders" are a common ingredient of ornament covers. Follow these steps for a basic ladder (shown in bugle beads but the same for cubes, triangles, etc.)

1. String on two beads.

2. Loop the thread back up through the first bead.

3. Pull the thread up so the two beads lie side by side.

4.   Run the thread back down through the second bead so that the thread is going in the first bead and out the second bead. Pull the thread down.

5. Add another bead, looping the thread back through the last bead.

6. Run the thread back through the bead you just added.

7. Keep adding beads till you have the desired length. Two basic steps: loop on a new bead, run the needle back out the new bead so you are ready for the next one.

Ladder with Tila (two-hole) beads.

A ladder with two-hole beads is the same as a basic ladder with one extra loop to get the thread coming out of the second hole in the new bead.

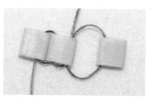

Tila Ornament

Material List

Tila Beads (Miyuki 2-hole beads)	44 pc
8/0 Triangle Seed Beads	180 pc
11/0 Rocaille	1824 pc
15/0 Rocaille	512 pc
4mm Crystal Bicones	8 pc
6mm Crystal Bicones	8 pc
4mm Pearls	8 pc
6mm Pearls	8 pc
Needle #10 Beading	
Size D Beading Thread	
Thread Conditioner	
2 1/2"-2 5/8" Ornament	

Start by making a ladder with the 44 Tila beads. See Chapter one.

Connect the two ends as if making another step on the ladder.

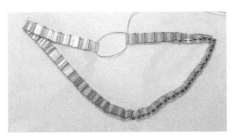

With needle coming out through the right side hole in a Tila bead, string on 2 15/0, 11/0, triangle, 11/0, 2 15/0.

Bring the needle up through the right side hole of the next Tila bead.

Repeat these diagonals all the way around.

With thread coming up from right side of Tila bead, string on 1 triangle and run thread down through left side hole of the Tila.

String on one more triangle and bring thread back up through same right side hole.

Run the thread back through the first triangle.

String on 15/0, 13 11/0, 15/0, triangle, 15/0, 13 11/0, 15/0, triangle.

Run the needle down through the 11th hole past where the thread is coming out (not the 11th bead; each bead has two holes), string on 1 triangle and come back up through the 10th hole.

Run the needle back through the triangle on top.

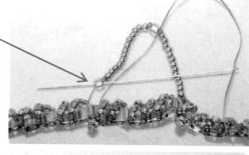

When you pull the thread tight this makes the first swag on the top side of the ornament cover.

Continue around the ornament, connecting your triangles through the 11th hole and back up through the 10th hole. When you get to the last swag, leave off the end triangle and run the thread back through the first triangle in the row.

Anchor the first round by running the needle back down through the Tila, through the triangle on the bottom, back up through the Tila and back through the top side triangle.

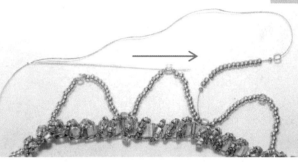

Start the second round by stringing on 15/0, 14 11/0, 15/0, triangle. Turn the needle back left to right through the center triangle of the 1st round.

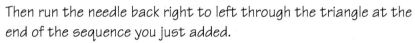

Then run the needle back right to left through the triangle at the end of the sequence you just added.

Complete the 1st swag by stringing on 15/0, 14 11/0, 15/0. Run the needle right to left through the triangle from the previous round.

Pull the thread down snug.

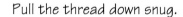

Continue around the cover until you reach the beginning point. Run the thread back up through the first string of beads so that the needle exits to the left of a center triangle.

7

Using 8 triangle beads, make a ladder coming off the two triangles in the swags.

With the thread exiting the top triangle, string on 3 15/0, run the needle through the next triangle, string on 3 15/0, and repeat down the ladder, exiting through the bottom triangle in the ladder.

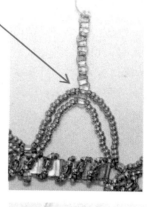

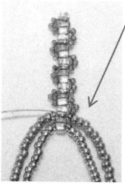

Repeat going back up the ladder so that you have loops on both sides.

String on 4 11/0 and 1 triangle. Using 7 more triangles, make a ladder going down and connect the ladder to the top triangle in the next swag.

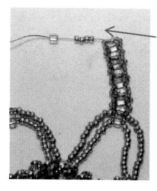

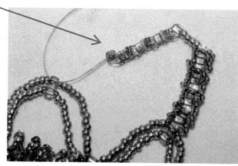

Run the needle back and forth through the ladder to get back to the top.

Make the loops of 15/0 down and back up on the ladder and string on 4 11/0. Continue making ladders with 4 11/0 between each until you reach the point of beginning.

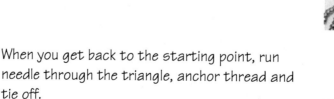

When you get back to the starting point, run needle through the triangle, anchor thread and tie off.

You have now completed the top half of the cover.

1st bottom swag:

Start a new thread exiting one of the triangles on the bottom side of the center Tila band. String on 15/0, 35 11/0, 15/0 and run the needle through the next triangle on the bottom.

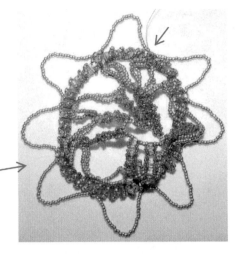

Continue around, exiting through the first triangle.

2nd bottom swag:

Add a triangle using the ladder stitch method. Exit through right side of triangle.

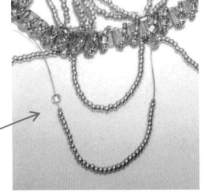

String on 15/0, 36 11/0, 15/0, triangle.

Attach triangle to triangle of 1st swag.

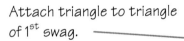

Continue around the cover exiting the 1st triangle.

Add another triangle to start next swag row.

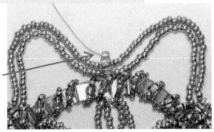

3rd bottom swag:

Make 3rd swag the same as 2nd swag but use 37 11/0.

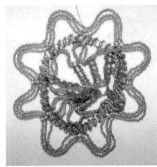

4th bottom swag with fringe:

String on 5 15/0, 7 11/0, 4mm crystal, 11/0, 15/0, 4mm pearl, 15/0, 11/0, 6mm crystal, 11/0, 15/0, 6mm pearl, 15/0.

Go around the bottom 15/0

Run the needle back up through all but the top 5 15/0.

String on 5 15/0 and run back through the triangle. Tighten thread up.

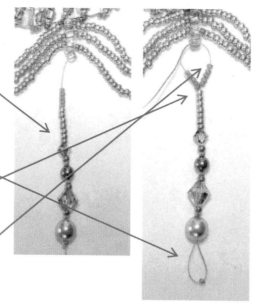

String on 5 15/0, 38 11/0, 5 15/0, triangle. Attach the triangle through the next triangle in the 3rd swag row as in last swag.

Continue around the cover adding a fringe sequence between each swag.

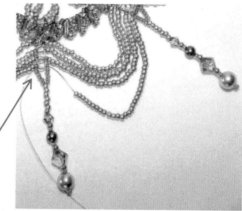

On the last swag, leave off the triangle and run the needle through the triangle at the beginning of the row. Tie off and bury the thread.

Your ornament cover is now complete. Experiment with different colors of ornaments and different color combinations of beads. Try using different drop beads and lengthening the fringe for a different look.

Elegant Crowned Ornament

Material List

6mm Bugle Beads	40 pc	
12mm Bugle Beads	20 pc	
11/0 color #1	673 pc	(designated as #1 in pattern)
11/0 color #2	190 pc	(designated as #2 in pattern)
15/0 match color #2	165 pc	
4mm Pearls	15 pc	
6mm Pearls	10 pc	
8mm Pearls	5 pc	
8mm Crystal Bicone	5 pc	
Needle #10 Beading		
Size D Beading Thread		
Thread Conditioner		
Ornament 2 1/2"-2 5/8"		

Crown:

Make a ladder with the 40 6mm bugle beads.
See Chapter 1.

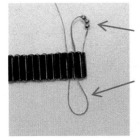

With the thread coming out of the end bugle bead, string on 3 15/0.

Run the thread down through 2nd bugle and back up through 3rd bugle. Pull thread tight.

Continue adding 15/0 beads across the top of the row, down one, up the next. This is a "picot" edge.

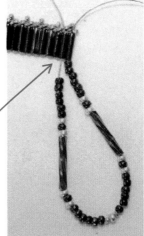

With needle exiting bottom of end bugle, string on 6 #1, #2, #1, #2, 12mm bugle, #2, #1, #2, 6 #1, 15/0, #2 (bottom bead), 15/0, 6 #1, #2, #1, #2, 12mm bugle, #2, #1, #2, 6 #1.

Run the needle back up through the next 6mm bugle at the top.

To get to the spot for the next loop, run the needle down the next bugle, up the next and down the next. This skips over two bugle beads.

String on 6 #1, #2, #1, #2, 4mm pearl, #2, #1, #2, 6 #1.

Run the needle up through the next bugle.

Skip over two bugles and out the next to make the 3rd loop.

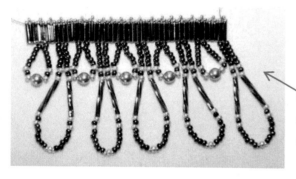

Continue making loops, alternating long and short, skipping over two bugle beads between each loop. Run the thread down and up at the end to exit the last bugle.

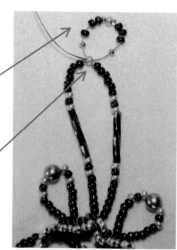

Fold the two ends together and sew back and forth, up and down through the bugles to make a circle with the ladder.

This completes the top section. Tie off and knot the thread ends.

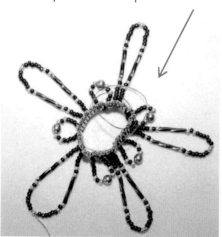

Begin a new thread, exiting through the 11/0 at the bottom of a long loop.

String on 15/0, 3 #1, 15/0, #2, 15/0, 3 #1, 15/0.

Run the needle back through the 11/0 where you started to make a loop.

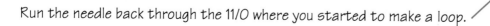

String on 15/0, 12 #1, #2, #1, #2, 4mm pearl, #2, #1, #2, 12 #1, 15/0.

Run the needle through the 11/0 at the bottom of the next long loop. Be careful not to twist the long loops.

Make another small loop.

Repeat the swag sequence.
Continue around the cover, adding a small loop between each swag. Exit through the 11/0 at the bottom of a small loop.

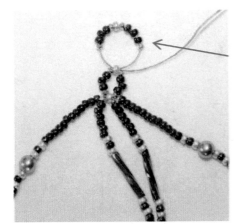

Make another small loop with the same sequence as the last round.

Make another swag with the same sequence as the last round except use a 6mm pearl.

Continue around the cover, alternating swags and loops.

Exit through the 11/0 at the bottom of a small loop.

The last round makes the fringe and the last row of swags.

String on 15/0, 3 #1, #2, #1, #2, 12mm bugle, #2, #1, #2, 15/0, #1, 4mm pearl, #2, #1, #2, 8mm crystal, #2, 8mm pearl, 15/0.

Run the needle around the bottom 15/0 and back up through the next 8 beads, exiting through the #1 just above the small pearl.

String on 15/0, #2, #1, #2, 12mm bugle, #2, #1, #2, 3 #1, 15/0.

Run the needle back through the 11/0 at the bottom of the small loop.

String on 15/0, 12 #1, #2, #1, #2, 6mm pearl, #2, #1, #2, 12 #1, 15/0.

Run the needle through the bottom 11/0 of the next small loop.

Continue alternating between fringe and swags all the way around.

Exit through the 11/0 at the bottom of the small loop where you started the round. Tie off and bury the thread back into the ornament, trim off excess thread and the cover is done.

Experiment with different color schemes, different colors of ornaments (all the examples in this book are on white ornaments only because they photograph better than most other colors), and different beads for the fringe. The one on the right used fire polished 8mm beads in the fringe instead of crystal.

Egyptian Collar Ornament

Material List

6mm Bugle Beads	96 pc	
12mm Bugle Beads	24 pc	
11/0 color #1	672 pc	(designated as #1 in the pattern)
11/0 color #2	516 pc	(designated as #2 in the pattern)
15/0 color #1	936 pc	
4mm Crystal Bicones	12 pc	
8mm Fire Polish Round	24 pc	
#10 Needle		
Size D Beading Thread		
Thread Conditioner		
2 1/2"-2 5/8" Ornament		

1st Round

String on 48 11/0 #1. Lay them in a circle and run the needle back around the circle to reinforce. Tie the two thread ends together.

2nd Round

With thread coming out of the 1st 11/0, string on 6mm bugle, #1, 6mm bugle.
Run the needle back through the 3rd 11/0 in the top ring, skipping over one 11/0. Thread will be coming out of 1st 11/0 and going through 3rd 11/0. (The loop twisted in the photo; the thread is coming out to the left.)

Continue making loops around the ring, 24 loops total.

3rd Round

Run the thread down a bugle and out through the 11/0 at the bottom of a loop from 2nd round.
String on 15/0, #1, 15/0.
Run needle through 11/0 at bottom of next loop.

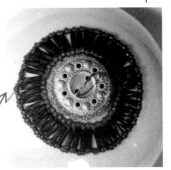

Continue around to complete the ring. Exit needle at center bead #1 from this round.

15

4th Round

String on 15/0, 2 #1. 3 #2, 5 #1, 3 #2, 2 #1, 15/0.
Run needle through the 11/0 at the center of next section of 3rd round.

Continue around the cover making 24 loops total.

Exit thread at the bottom center 11/0 of the first loop.

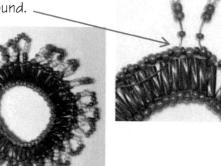

5th Round

String on 15/0, 3 #1, 15/0.
Run needle through 11/0 at center of next loop.

Continue around to complete the ring.
Exit at center 11/0 of first loop from this round.

6th Round

String on 15/0, 6mm bugle, 2 15/0, 3 #2, 2 15/0, 6mm bugle, 15/0.
Run needle through center 11/0 of next section from 5th round.

String on one 15/0 and run needle back through the second bugle you just strung.

String on the next loop with just the center beads and the second bugle bead: 2 15/0, 3 #2, 2 15/0, 6mm bugle, 15/0.

Run through next center 11/0, add the 15/0 and run back through the bugle bead.

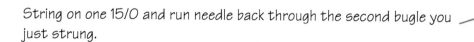

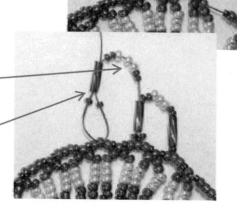

When you get back to the beginning of the round, run the needle back through the first bugle bead from the first loop.

String on one 15/0 and run the needle back through the 11/0 and 15/0 at the top of the bugle (shown below the bugle here) and back through the bugle bead.

Exit the thread through the center 11/0 of the first loop.

7th Round

String on 15/0, 2 #1, 3 #2, 5 #1, 3 #2, 2 #1, 15/0.

Run the needle back through the 11/0 the thread came out of at the beginning of the loop plus the 11/0 next to it.

String on 3 15/0.
Run the needle through the 1st two 11/0 in the next section.

Pull thread up to make a loop plus a link.

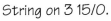

Continue making these loops with links between all the way around.

Exit thread through the center 11/0 of the first loop.

8th Round

String on 15/0, 4 #1, 15/0.

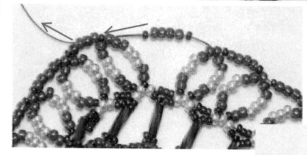

Run needle through the center 11/0 of the next loop from the 7th round.

Continue around the cover. At the last set, run the needle through the center 11/0 where you started plus through the first four beads you added at the beginning of the round (15/0, 3 #1).

9th Round

String on 2 15/0, 6mm bugle, 3 15/0, 3 #2, 3 15/0, 6mm bugle, 2 15/0.

Run the needle through the *two* center 11/0 from the 8th round.

String on 2 15/0 and run the needle back through the last bugle.

String on 3 15/0, 3 #2, 3 15/0, 6mm bugle, 2 15/0. Run needle through the two center 11/0 of next section.

String on 2 15/0 and run back through the last bugle.

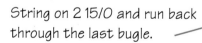
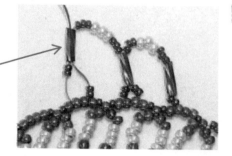

Continue around the cover.

At the end of the round, string on 3 15/0, 3 #2, 3 15/0. Run the needle down the first bugle from the first loop.

18

Run the needle through the two 15/0 at the top of the bugle, plus through the center two 11/0.

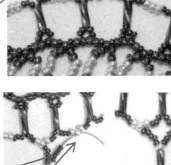

String on 2 15/0.
Run needle back through the bugle, 3 15/0, and 2 #2.

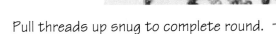

Pull threads up snug to complete round.

10th (final) Round

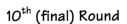

String on 5 15/0, #2, 12mm bugle, #2, 4mm bicone, #2, 8mm, #2, 15/0.

Run the needle around the bottom 15/0 and back up through all but the last 5 15/0.

String on 5 15/0.
Run needle through center 11/0 of next loop from 9th round.

Continue around the row, alternating fringe with and without the 4mm bicone as shown at far right.

Tie off and bury threads.

These samples are basically one color with a gold accent but you can try using different combinations with more variety of color.

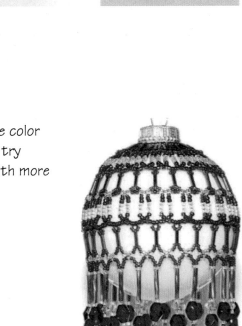

Belted Ornament

Material List

6mm Bugle Beads	110 pc
3mm Fire Polish Rounds	190 pc
15/0 Rocailles	320 pc
4mm Crystal Roundels	30 pc
11/0 Rocaillies	105 pc
6mm Crystal Bicone	10 pc
Tear Drops	5 pc
#10 Beading Needle	
Size D Beading Thread	
Thread Conditioners	
2 1/2"-2 5/8" Ornament	

Count out 40 6mm bugles and make them into a ladder.
See Getting Started.

String on 12 3mm fire polish with a 15/0 between each bead and at each end.
Then string on bugle, 15/0, 6mm bicone, 11/0, 4mm roundel, 11/0, 3mm f.p., 11/0, 6mm bicone, 11/0, 3mm f.p., 11/0, 4mm roundel, 11/0, tear drop, 15/0.

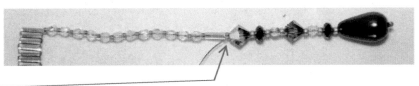

Go around the 15/0 at the end and run the needle back up through the next 13 beads and out the top of the first 6mm bicone.

String on 15/0, bugle. Run the needle back down the first bugle.

Snug the thread up and run it back up through the bugle you just added.

String on 15/0, 3mm f.p., 15/0, 3mm f.p. Run needle up through the 3rd 15/0 above the bugle bead.

String on 3mm f.p., 15/0, 3mm f.p., skip over one 15/0 and run the needle up through the next 15/0.

Keep repeating the last step until you reach the top. Finish the sequence with a 15/0 at the end and run the needle through the 2nd bugle in the top ladder.

String on 3 15/0 and run the needle down the next bugle and back up the next. Repeat three more times and end with thread out the bottom. (This is a "picot" edge.)

Continue across the ladder making a total of five drops with picot along the top edge.

The last fringe will <u>not</u> be at the end.

To finish off the top picot and connect the ends: String on 3 15/0.

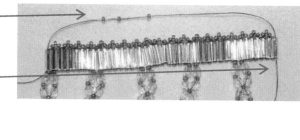

Run the needle down through the end bugle on the other end of the ladder.

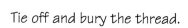

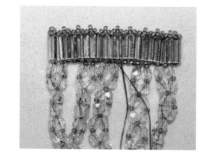

Run the needle back up and down through these two end bugles to secure the top ring.

Tie off and bury the thread.

Start a new thread on one of the bugles in one of the fringe.

Count out 6 bugles and make a ladder coming out from the existing bugle.

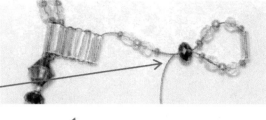

String on 15/0, 3mm f.p., 11/0, 3mm f.p., 15/0, 4mm roundel, 15/0, 3mm f.p., 11/0, 3mm f.p., 15/0, bugle, 15/0, 3mm f.p., 11/0, 3mm f.p., 15/0.

Run the needle back through the roundel.

String on 15/0, 3mm f.p., 11/0, 3mm f.p., 15/0.

Run the needle back up through the end bugle, forming a figure 8.

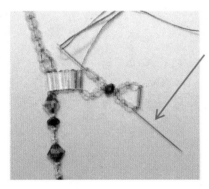

Run the needle diagonally through the figure 8 and back up through the bugle at the end of the figure 8.

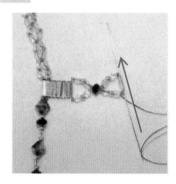

Count out 5 more bugles and make a ladder connecting the end bugle from the figure 8 with the next bugle in the next fringe. Be careful to select the correct bugle from the fringe or the fringe will be twisted.

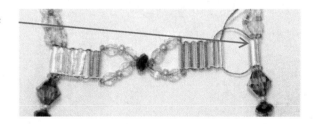

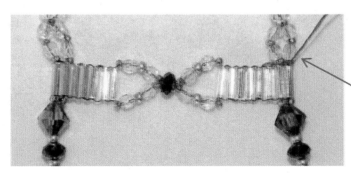

Run the needle down and up through the two bugles in the fringe so that the thread comes out the second bugle.

Repeat the ladder and figure 8 sequence around the cover.

Exit the needle out the bottom of the bugle bead next to a fringe.

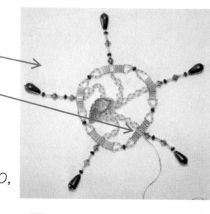

String on 5 15/0, 3 11/0, 3mm f.p., 11/0, 4mm roundel, 11/0, 3mm f.p., 11/0, 4mm roundel, 11/0, 3mm f.p., 11/0, 4mm roundel, 11/0, 3mm f.p., 3 11/0, 5 15/0.

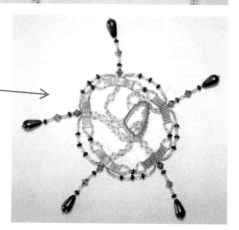

Pull up swag and run the needle up and down through the bugles to come out the bottom side of the 1st bugle on the other side of the next fringe.

Continue around the cover until all sections have a swag between the fringe.

Tie off and bury threads.

Try using different colors and experiment with different fringe beads. The cover on the right looks great on a gold ball (the 3mm f.p. are apollo gold color and the bugles are copper lined —shown on white because the gold didn't show up well in a photo).

Cubed Ornament

Material List

1.8mm Cubes	60 pc
3mm Cubes	78 pc
15/0 Rocailles	1488 pc
11/0 Rocailles	648 pc
12mm Bugle Beads	36 pc
3mm Crystal Bicones	120 pc
4mm Pearls	18 pc
6mm Pearls	18 pc
#10 Beading Needle	
Size D Beading Thread	
Thread Conditioner	
2 1/2" - 2 5/8" Ornament	

1st Round

String on 3mm cube, 7 15/0, 1.8mm cube, 7 15/0. Repeat the sequence until you have 12 large and 12 small cubes, ending with 7 15/0.

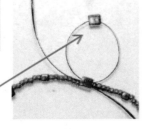

Run the needle through the 3mm cube at the beginning to make a circle.

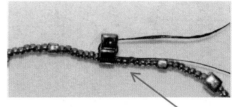

Pull thread snug.

2nd through 5th Round

Add on a 3mm cube, as in making a ladder.

Tie the two thread ends together and run the needle back through the new cube.

String on 7 15/0, 1.8mm cube.

Loop the thread back through the 1.8mm cube in the first round and back through the new cube.

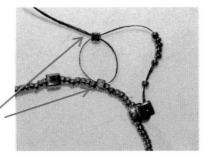

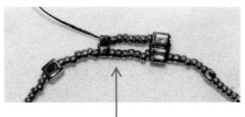

Pull snug.

Continue the sequence of 7 15/0, cube, alternating between 3mm and 1.8mm cubes to match the previous row.

At the end of a round leave off the cube at the end of the sequence and add a new cube to start the next round.
(The direction of work will change each time you add a cube to start a new round.)

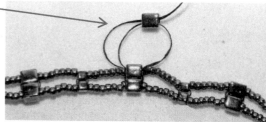

Complete 4 rows and start a 5th.

On the 5th row, add a loop of beads to _every other_ 3mm cube (6 loops total, not 12).
For the loop, string on 3 15/0, 11/0, bicone. 15/0, 6mm pearl, 15/0, bicone, 11/0, 3 15/0.
*Note: this small pearl loop on every other cube is not shown in some photos.

6th Round

Add a 3mm cube.

String on 5 15/0, 10 11/0, bicone, 4mm pearl, bicone, 10 11/0, 5 15/0, 3mm cube.

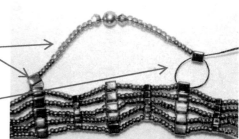

Loop thread back through the 2nd 3mm cube from the 5th round.

Complete the round, leaving off the last cube and running the needle through the cube at the beginning of the row as shown in 2nd round.

7th Round

Add a 3mm cube.

String on 5 15/0, 12 11/0, bicone, 4mm pearl, bicone, 12 11/0, 5 15/0, 3mm cube.

Connect to next 3mm cube.

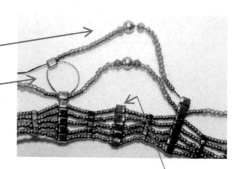

Complete the round, leaving off the last cube and running the needle through the cube at the beginning of the row as shown in 2nd round.

(Small pearl loop here)

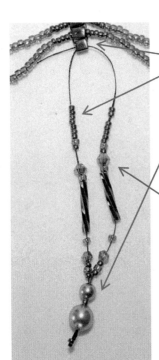

8th Round

Add a 3mm cube.

String on 7 15/0, 11/0, 15/0, bicone, 11/0, bugle, 11/0, bicone, 15/0, 11/0, 15/0, 4mm pearl, 15/0, 6mm pearl, 15/0.

Run the needle around the bottom 15/0 and back up, coming out at the top of the 4mm pearl.

String on 15/0, 11/0, 15/0, bicone, 11/0, bugle, 11/0, bicone, 15/0, 11/0, 7 15/0.

Run the needle through the cube you just added at the top of the fringe. Tighten up the fringe.

To make the swag between the fringes, string on 5 15/0, 15 11/0, bicone, 6mm pearl, bicone, 15 11/0, 5 15/0, 3mm cube.

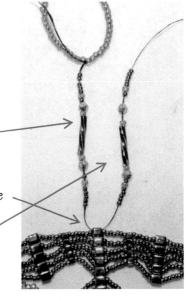

Loop the thread back through the next 3mm cube in the last round to secure.

Continue around the cover until you have 6 fringe and 6 swags in the bottom round, leaving off the last cube and running the needle back through the first 3mm cube. Tie off and bury the thread.

This completes the bottom section of the cover. Set it aside for the moment.

Top

Start a new thread.
String on 48 11/0.
Form into a circle and run the needle back through the circle to reinforce. Tie the ends together.

String on 5 15/0, 11/0, 15/0, bicone, 11/0, bugle, 11/0, bicone, 15/0, 11/0, 5 15/0.

Run the needle through a 3mm cube from the bottom row that you had set aside.

String on the same sequence again.

To connect to the top ring, skip over one 11/0 and run needle through next three 11/0 and out.

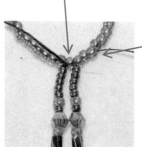

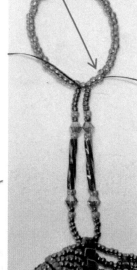

String on the same sequence again, connecting to the next 3mm cube in the bottom section.

Continue around until you have 12 connections with 3 11/0 between each at the top ring.

Tie off and bury the thread.

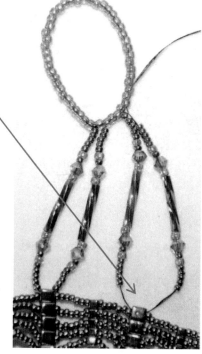

This ornament cover uses a lot of 15/0 rocailles but using larger beads just doesn't come out with the same nice drape.

Made in the USA
Las Vegas, NV
15 June 2023

73493720R00021